Changes in You and Me

A Book about Puberty, *Mostly for Girls*

Paulette Bourgeois and Kim Martyn

Illustrated by Louise Phillips

KEY PORTER BOOKS

Library and Archives Canada Cataloguing in Publication

Bourgeois, Paulette
    Changes in you and me : a book about puberty mostly for girls / Paulette Bourgeois. —
Rev. / by Kim Martyn

Includes bibliographical references and index.
ISBN 1-55263-670-4

1. Puberty—Juvenile literature. 2. Sex instruction for girls—Juvenile literature.
I. Martyn, Kim II. Title.

HQ51.B69 2005   j613.9'55   C2005-900900-4

The publisher gratefully acknowledges the support of the Canada Council for the Arts and
the Ontario Arts Council for its publishing program. We acknowledge the support of the
Government of Ontario through the Ontario Media Development Corporation's Ontario
Book Initiative.

We acknowledge the financial support of the Government of Canada through the Book
Publishing Industry Development Program (BPIDP) for our publishing activities.

Key Porter Books Limited
Six Adelaide Street East, Tenth Floor
Toronto, Ontario
Canada M5C 1H6

www.keyporter.com

Text design: Peter Maher
Electronic formatting: Jean Lightfoot Peters

Printed and bound in Canada

05 06 07 08 09 6 5 4 3 2 1

Acknowledgments

The authors would like to acknowledge all the wonderful adolescents, parents, teachers and health professionals who so thoughtfully answered many difficult and challenging questions. Friends and their children were forthcoming with anecdotes, questions and suggestions. We are grateful to Key Porter for their full support of a book about puberty that "tells it all" candidly and with humor. Linda Pruessen's vision for the revised edition was right on.

We are grateful to Dr. Martin Wolfish and Dr. David Lloyd, consultants in pediatrics and adolescent medicine, who reviewed the original manuscript and made valuable comments. We also thank Father Bob Moran, Mary Scandrett, Erica Glossop, Elizabeth Anne Gordon, Jane Somerville, Patrick Crean, Jennifer Glossop, Bettina Federspiel and Lyba Spring.

Note to the Reader

Welcome to your life! We've written this book for youth who want to know a bit more about this time called *puberty*. In this book we try to give you some information about the physical, emotional and social changes that people go through during puberty. As you can see from the title, this book focuses mainly on girls. (There is a section about what happens to boys as well, in case you're curious.) Everybody will go through puberty in their own way, at their own speed, so some information in this book you already know, some you may not be interested in until later.

When talking about bodies and sexual matters people use lots of different kinds of words—slang, dictionary, polite and baby talk. In this book we use mostly dictionary or medical words so that you'll know the "real" terms. Since you've been taught the dictionary words for other parts of your body, like "elbow," you may as well know the words for the reproductive and sexual parts, too!

There may be words you don't understand or cannot pronounce. Look in the glossary at the end of the book for an explanation of the words that appear in *italics*.

If some of the language or content in this book grosses you out or offends you, we apologize. However, we think that with a topic as important as this, it's a good idea to be as clear as possible.

Note to Parents, Caregivers and Other Caring Adults

While this book was written for girls ages 9 to 13, you may also find some of it interesting! As we state above in the Note to the Reader, we apologize in advance for any offense taken regarding the language or content used in the text. We think that it is important that youth clearly understand this information and at times that means including terms that are commonly used. We have also included topics that may be beyond a child's years at this point but may not be a couple of years from now. Please see For More Information on page 59.

Contents

1 A Time of Change

Every girl and boy goes through a stage of life called *adolescence*. This weird and wonderful time exists between childhood and adulthood. As you pass through it, you experience changes: you become more independent; you start to sort out your feelings about yourself, and your friends and family. You also make decisions about how you want to look, things like smoking or drinking and what to do when you like someone. You will experience the physical changes of growing up. This book is about all these changes. It is about *puberty*.

You probably already know a lot about your body and about boys' bodies and even about the changes of puberty. Here's a quiz for you to test yourself.

True or False?

1. Puberty is the same as sexuality.	T	F
2. It takes years for all the changes to happen.	T	F
3. Getting your period is the first sign of puberty.	T	F
4. Your hair gets darker during puberty.	T	F
5. Girls who start puberty early have bigger breasts.	T	F
6. Girls don't talk with their dads about these changes.	T	F
7. If you eat vitamins, you can speed up puberty.	T	F
8. Most girls start puberty before age 10.	T	F
9. Its only girls who get mood swings during puberty.	T	F
10. Some girls are age 16 when their periods start.	T	F

ANSWERS: 1.F, 2.T, 3.F, 4.T, 5.F, 6.F, 7.F, 8.F, 9.F, 10.T

Puberty and Sexuality

Puberty is different from *sexuality*. Puberty means the changes that happen inside and outside our bodies as we mature so that, if we want to, we can reproduce when we're older.

Sexuality is a huge part of who you are, from the moment you're born until the end of your life. It has to do with *gender*, being *female* or *male*. Of course it includes the reproductive parts of our body, which are needed to make babies. For girls this means the *ovaries*, a *uterus*, the *vulva* and the *vagina*. Sexuality also has to do with how comfortable you are with yourself and your body. Another part has to do with whom we become sexually attracted to, called *orientation*. And the part that makes many young people laugh is the sexual feelings we get and may, later on, share with another person. Some people refer to this aroused feeling as being *horny*.

People have *sexual intercourse* for pleasure and to make babies. Some common words for sexual intercourse are making love, *sex*, having sex, doing it, sleeping together and going all the way. There are many more slang terms you've likely heard! Before two people have sexual intercourse, they usually kiss and touch each other above and below the waist. This is sometimes called *making out* or *fooling around*.

As we mentioned, sexuality isn't just about sex. As a baby you needed to be touched and held just to survive. As you grew, you learned the kind of touches that made you feel warm and loved and the kind of touches you didn't like. Hugs can feel great. But a hug when you don't want one feels uncomfortable. Sometimes even nice touches turn into uncomfortable touches. Have you ever been tickled and yelled "Stop!" but the person kept tickling you? Not fun.

What Changes Happen in Puberty?

Stage 1.

Your body is growing quickly. Perhaps your arms, legs and feet seem "too long." You might be tired and want to sleep a lot. Your hips and thighs get wider, and so your waist seems smaller.

Stage 2.

Your *nipples* get puffy and rounder. *Breasts* start to grow, often as a lump under the nipple. *Pubic hair* begins to grow around the vulva. You will notice a bit of whitish fluid or *discharge* on the inside of your underpants. This comes out of the vagina.

Stage 3.

Hair starts to grow in your armpits. The hair on your arms and legs will also get darker and thicker. Soft upper lip hair often develops.

Stage 4.

You sweat more and the sweat smells stronger. Your skin and hair produce more oil, often resulting in pimples.

Stage 5.

You may start having more sexual and romantic feelings. Your *period* starts. This is called *menstruation* (more about this later). There are also changes in your brain, so that you can now think about things in more complex ways.

When Does Puberty Start?

Something I like about the way I look now is.............. (name at least one thing, even if you don't want to write it down).

Puberty takes a long time from beginning to end, about three to five years. There is no "right age" and there's no way to speed it up or slow it down.

Puberty starts for most girls sometime between 8 and 13 years old. No two girls go through puberty in exactly the same way. In every sixth grade classroom, there are girls who are nearing the end of puberty and girls who are just beginning. That's usual.

If you start puberty much before the age of 8, or show no signs of it by the time you are 13, your parent can mention it to your doctor.

What Will I Look Like?

What determines how you will look when you grow up? How tall you become, hair color, the size of your breasts, skin type and your overall shape depend mostly on *heredity*. This means the *genes* you got from your birth parents. For example, if all your blood relatives are tall, it is likely you will be, too. If all your relatives are short, there's a good chance that's how you'll look when you're an adult.

Aside from genetics, our looks also depend on what food we eat and how active we are. There's more on this in Chapter 6.

During puberty, parts of your body grow at different times, so be patient if your nose or toes seem to have sprung ahead of the rest of you.

As you know, some people go to a lot of effort to change the way they naturally look. Unfortunately we hear lots of put-downs about people's bodies—their weight, height, hair, skin and clothes. This is especially true for girls. These comments put us all under a lot of pressure to look a certain way. If you watch TV and look at magazines you'll notice the actors and models almost all have a certain "look." They are mainly young and slim with clear, light-colored skin. Many of the guys are muscular and the females have perky breasts. Everyone knows this isn't how real people look. We come in all ages, shapes and sizes. The challenge is to like what you have and not pay too much attention to the pressure you may feel to change yourself. Sure it's fun to make yourself look different in some way, just don't lose yourself!

How Will I Feel?

Most girls ask, "Am I normal? Does anyone else feel this way?" The answer is almost always yes, even though you think you are acting, feeling or growing in a way that seems different from other people your age.

When you begin to notice that you're changing you may feel like letting others know, or you may not. Some girls feel kind of proud or happy, others feel shy or even wish the changes weren't happening. How you feel depends on lots of things, particularly on other people's reactions. If you are constantly teased or bullied because you are changing somewhat faster or slower than others, it's hard to feel excited. Sometimes even family members make such a big deal about puberty that it can be embarrassing. However, if the people around you react appropriately, it's much easier to feel okay.

You might think you are the only person feeling weird about puberty. You're not alone! If there is one common thing about puberty, it is that almost everybody worries about being normal. Remember that everybody goes through puberty in their own way, at their own speed.

The chances are that everything you are experiencing is perfectly normal. And, hopefully, you don't have to worry about being teased or bullied. But if you are worried, or are being bothered by others, talk with someone in your family, a doctor, a teacher, a youth leader or a counselor. There are also hotline numbers on page 59 that may be of help. Of course girls often go to their friends first. This is fine, it's just that people your age may not have all the information they need. And while it's also true that adults sure don't know everything, they'll usually do their best to help.

Talk It Over

Talking with your mom or dad (yes, your dad!) may be helpful. It also makes it more likely that they will trust you as you get older and want more freedom. Here are a couple of questions you can ask them if they are shy:

1. "When you were growing up, how did you find out about all this puberty stuff?"
2. "As a teen, what kind of skin did you have—clear or lots of pimples?"

2 The Inside Story

You'll know puberty has started when you begin to show the obvious signs—underarm and pubic hair, a whitish fluid from the vagina and developing breasts. But many of the changes of puberty happen inside your body, in your brain, under your skin and in your *reproductive organs*.

Internal Sex Organs

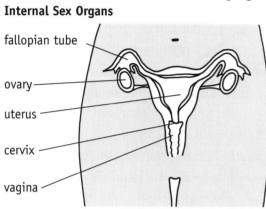

fallopian tube

ovary

uterus

cervix

vagina

The reproductive organs have many names, including *genitals* and sex organs. Some of them are on the inside, and others are on the outside. They have been growing, along with every other part of your body, since you were born.

Your uterus, *cervix*, vagina, ovaries and *fallopian tubes* are protected by a wide ring of bones called the pelvic bones. The uterus, where a baby grows, is about the size of your fist. If you put your fist below below your belly button, that's about where your uterus is in your body. When a woman becomes *pregnant*, her uterus can stretch to fit the growing baby inside.

The lower part of the uterus is the cervix. During a period, the special blood flows from the uterus through the cervix and out the vagina. The opening to the cervix is small, but it stretches during childbirth.

Your vagina, the passageway from the uterus to outside your body, is a narrow tube of muscle, but it stretches during sexual intercourse so a *penis* can fit inside. The vagina also expands during birth so a baby can travel through it.

Your ovaries are each the size of a thumbnail, even though they contain hundreds of thousands of *ova* (eggs). A single egg is called an ovum. The two *fallopian tubes* carry the ova to the uterus. They are as thin as a strand of spaghetti.

The sex organs on the outside of your body have a name other than your "private parts"! They are called the vulva. Some people call the area the vagina, but that's only one opening. The vulva includes the soft mound of tissue that covers the pubic bone; the *inner and outer lips*

External Genitals

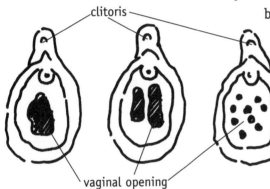

pubic hair

clitoris

urethral opening

vaginal opening

anus

('cause that's what they look like), which together are called the *labia*; the *clitoris* and the vaginal opening. The *bladder* is where *urine* is stored. The *urethra*, the opening where urine comes out, and the *anus*, where *bowel movements* come out, are also found here.

So girls have three openings down there. Guys just have two.

Before puberty, girls have no hair on their vulva, and it is difficult to see that there are two "lips" surrounding the urethra and vaginal opening. During puberty, your outside genitals become more noticeable. Unless you are very flexible, the easiest way to see what's going on is to have a look in a mirror. The shape and color of the inner lips is quite different in different girls.

Types of Hymens

clitoris

vaginal opening

The *hymen* is a thin piece of skin inside the vaginal opening. It may become more noticeable during puberty. Some girls are born without a hymen, while in other girls it may be fairly thick. Or it may cover just a small part of the opening. For many of us the hymen gets stretched when we are active, participating in activities such as riding a bike or doing gymnastics. Using a tampon may stretch the hymen as well. During sexual intercourse for the first time, if the hymen is thicker and has not been stretched there may be discomfort. But most of the time this is not the case.

The clitoris is a small, highly sensitive organ that gives females of all ages a pleasurable feeling when it is stimulated. Some people say it is an excited or shivery feeling. However, it can also hurt a lot if accidentally hit. The small outside part of the clitoris can be seen where the lips of the vulva join, above the urethra. The inside part is like a root that runs under the muscles along both sides of the vagina.

Raging Hormones

Some Important Glands

pituitary

thyroid

adrenal

ovary

Hormones are powerful chemical messengers in your body. They are made in special *glands* and travel through the bloodstream. Each hormone has a specific job. When you are about to run a race, before you start, you feel your heart pounding and your body suddenly bursting with energy. This happens because a certain hormone is released. There are different hormones that make puberty happen.

Deep inside your brain there is an organ smaller than a marble called the *pituitary gland*. It acts as a master switch and "turns on" your body to make sex hormones for the first time.

Boys and girls both make the same sex hormones—*estrogen*, *progesterone* and *testosterone*. Girls make lots of estrogen and progesterone and very little testosterone, while it is the opposite for boys.

You can thank hormones for making your oil and *sweat glands* work overtime, giving you stronger body odor and more oily skin and hair. They can change the way you feel, too. You might have sudden mood changes. Or more sexual thoughts about other people.

Estrogen tells your body to develop more fatty tissue around your hips, thighs and breasts. Both estrogen and progesterone are responsible for a monthly cycle called the menstrual cycle—your period. Stay tuned for more about that in Chapter 5.

3 Sex and Pregnancy

From the time we're born we are all sexual beings. Once puberty happens, not only do you have the potential to reproduce, but you may find you think more about romance and sexual stuff. You may wonder what it's like to be in love and kiss somebody. Sexual thoughts, fantasies, curiosity and *masturbation*, or self-exploration, are common for girls and guys as they grow up.

Masturbation/ Self-Exploration

Throughout our lives we try to figure out how our bodies work and what feels nice.

Some women and girls touch their breasts and genitals because it gives them feelings of sexual pleasure. This is called masturbation. You'll hear lots of jokes about this, especially from guys, who may call it *"jerking off," "jacking off,"* or "playing with yourself." Unlike some stories you may have heard, self-exploration won't cause any physical harm. Some adults and religious teachings say that this kind of self-pleasuring is not okay. Part of growing up involves deciding what you believe and feel comfortable doing, or not doing. It's your body, so it's up to you.

When Can You Have Sex?

It is possible for people to have sexual intercourse and make babies as soon as boys make *sperm* and girls start to *ovulate*. But does this mean it's a good time to start? You're likely saying "No way!" And you're right. You'll read more about the serious side of sex in Chapter 9.

Sexual Orientation

<u>Transsexual</u> refers to a person who looks like one gender on the outside but feels like the other gender...complicated!

Whom you are emotionally and sexually attracted to is referred to as your orientation. This is different than your gender, which refers to being male or female. People who are mainly attracted to people of the opposite sex are called *heterosexual* or *straight*. Those who are mainly attracted to the same sex are called *homosexual*, with *lesbian* as the term for female and *gay* as the term for males. And just to make it even more complex, there are people who are interested in both men and women. The term for this is *bisexual*.

People of all orientations may fall in love and spend their lives together. When people decide to share themselves in a sexual way they may hug, touch, kiss and have sex with each other. The big difference is that if there isn't a penis and a vagina, then that kind of intercourse doesn't happen. And without sperm and an egg the couple cannot make their own child.

People often ask the question, "Why are some people gay?" Nobody really knows the answer. The same goes for the question, "Why are most people straight?" What we do know is that we do not choose our orientation; it's something that just is the way it is.

When we grow up it is common to have a strong attraction to other females, such as a girlfriend, teacher or actor. As you get older, these feelings may continue, or not. If you are ever confused about thoughts and feelings you have as you get older please talk to an adult you trust, or call a talk line for youth. Often what you're experiencing is perfectly normal—just new to you!

a good question!

"Is there any other way of getting pregnant than having you-know-what?"
—GRADE 5 STUDENT

When you're younger you can't imagine having sex, even if you want to have kids. Don't worry; those feelings generally disappear once you get older. However, some people can't get pregnant through sexual intercourse, and so they may get some extra help. Artificial insemination is when sperm is put into a woman's vagina. In vitro fertilization occurs when the egg is removed by a doctor and fertilized by a sperm outside of the woman's body. It is then put in the uterus to grow.

Having Sex—Making Love

sperm + seminal
fluid = semen

Sexual intercourse between a woman and a man is usually the way people make babies. It is also a way they can give and get physical pleasure.

When two people are ready and want to be as close as possible to each other, they may have sexual intercourse. They touch, stroke and kiss each other until the man's penis becomes larger and erect and the woman's vagina becomes wet and slippery from special fluids her body makes.

The man slides his penis inside the woman's vagina and moves his penis in and out until *semen*, called *come*, spurts out. This is called *ejaculation*. The sensation that usually accompanies an ejaculation is called an *orgasm*. The woman may also have an orgasm. Once the man has ejaculated, his penis will again become smaller and soft, and will slip out of the vagina.

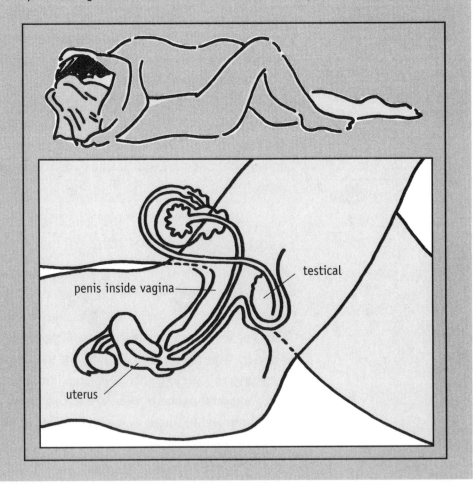

penis inside vagina

testical

uterus

Fertilization: How Pregnancy Starts

You've likely heard about females making ova or "eggs," which are needed to make a baby. And you probably already know that guys make sperm cells. These cells carry the codes for creating human life. These are called genes. The genes contain messages for cells about how they should grow and act. The ovum has the genes from the mother. A sperm cell carries genes from the father.

The ovum is the largest human cell, the only one you can see with your eyes. This is about the size of a human ovum, or egg.

During sexual intercourse, semen is ejaculated into the vagina. About 400 million sperm race to fertilize the ovum (egg). The journey takes hours, and most of the sperm die off before they reach the fallopian tubes. And if there is no ovum in the tube at that time, then there is no pregnancy.

As soon as one sperm enters the egg, no other sperm can enter. The sperm and the egg join together. The egg is *fertilized*. This is also called *conception*. The fertilized egg then travels down the tube and attaches to the inside of the uterus. From now until it is nine weeks old, it is called an *embryo*.

How Does a Woman Know She's Pregnant?

Since the embryo is attached inside the uterus, a woman stops getting her period when she is pregnant (although stress, intense exercise or dieting can stop menstruation, too). She may feel tired, have tender breasts, pee more often and feel nauseated (want to throw up). However, lots of women don't feel much different for quite a while.

The only sure way for somebody to know they are pregnant is to take a urine test. These are available at a doctor's office or clinic, or for sale at drugstores (although these are less accurate than a test at your doctor's office).

Being Pregnant

You often hear people say that the baby is growing in the mother's stomach, but of course that's not true! It's growing in a special place—the uterus.

The embryo grows quickly inside a sac filled with *amniotic fluid*. Here it floats, kicks and sleeps. It gets oxygen and nutrients and gets rid of its body waste through the *placenta*, an organ it shares with the mother. The embryo is attached to the placenta by the *umbilical cord*. Because the embryo totally depends on what comes from the mother, it's **very important** that she eat well and avoid chemicals and drugs, such as alcohol.

After nine weeks of growing, the embryo is called a *fetus*. It is the size of a peanut, and it has a bulgy head, internal organs, tiny arms and legs, fingers and a face.

12 weeks   24 weeks   40 weeks

Giving Birth

About nine months after fertilization, the baby is ready to be born. The mother's uterus is a powerful muscle. It tightens and relaxes until the baby is pushed out of the uterus. The opening in the cervix expands until it is wide enough for the baby's head. This is called labor—which is a good word since it means "work." Labor is exciting and tiring. Women are encouraged to focus on deep breathing and relaxing during labor. There are also certain positions, massage techniques and medicines to help with the birth process.

Usually, the baby's head comes out first, then the rest of the body slides out. The blood supply from the umbilical cord shuts off, and blood races to the lungs so that the baby can breathe. The umbilical cord, which has no feeling, is cut. The placenta and cord are also pushed out of the mother's body because they are no longer needed. After a few days, the remaining bit of the cut umbilical cord still attached to the baby's belly falls off. The scar that is left is called a belly button, or navel.

Some babies are born by *cesarean section* because they cannot be born through the vagina. The mother is given an anesthetic to numb her lower body, an incision (cut) is made through her uterus, the baby is lifted out and then the mom gets stitches.

Do you know the story of your birth? Ask someone about it!

a good question!

"Does having a baby hurt?"
—MIRANDA, AGE 10

For most women, delivering a baby *does* hurt, but not like when you have an accident. The labor pains come mostly from cramping in the muscles of the uterus that are working so hard to push the baby out. But it's like the cramp you may get in your leg when running hard—you just try and focus on finishing!

About Twins

There are two kinds of twins: fraternal and identical. Fraternal twins do not necessarily look alike while identical twins are, well, identical! Sometimes, two eggs are released into the fallopian tubes at ovulation. They are each fertilized by a different sperm. Two separate embryos, each with its own placenta, start to develop. These are fraternal twins.

Identical twins develop when one egg divides into two identical halves soon after fertilization. They share a placenta. The babies are born one at a time, often through a vaginal birth.

Conjoined or Siamese babies are identical twins that did not fully separate.

Identical Twins   **Fraternal Twins**

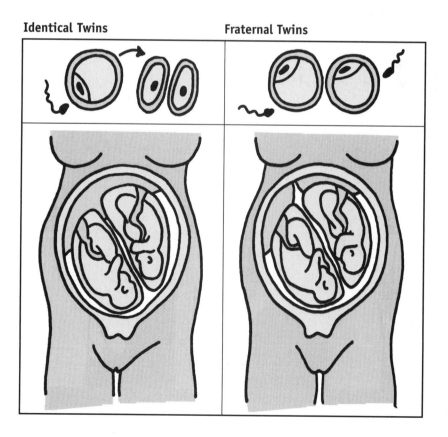

Miscarriage

Sometimes a woman is pregnant and things are not going as they should inside. Her body will end the pregnancy with a *miscarriage*, or spontaneous abortion. It will be as though she's having a very heavy period. This usually happens within the first three months, but it may be so early that she hasn't even discovered that she is pregnant yet. One in four pregnancies ends this way. If she wants to, the woman can go ahead and get pregnant again in a short while. A *stillbirth* is when the fetus dies when it is mostly made but not born yet. The delivery happens, but the baby is not alive. Fortunately, this does not happen very often.

4 Breasts and Pubic Hair

Before puberty, boys' and girls' chests look alike. They are smooth with small raised nipples. But when puberty starts, one of the first changes in girls is breast development.

The inside of the breast is made up of fatty tissue and many milk-producing glands called *mammary glands*. If a woman has a baby, breasts produce milk for feeding the infant. Humans have two breasts so that we can make enough milk for twins. Dogs make enough for 10 puppies or more!

Nipples—even those of boys—have a network of nerves that make them very sensitive. That's why, when it is cold, or when the nipples are touched, or when a person is thinking about something sexy or exciting, the nipples become harder and erect, or pointy.

How Breasts Develop

As with everything else in puberty, your body has its own timetable for developing breasts. The size of your breasts and the size and color of your nipples partially depend on genetics—what you inherit.

It takes three to five years from the time your breasts start to bud for them to grow to their full size. Since it happens slowly, you will have time to get used to the feel of your more grown-up body.

Most girls notice their chests changing when they are around 9 to 11 years old. Of course, it can be earlier or later. The final size of your breasts has nothing to do with the age when you started to develop. A girl who starts developing breasts when she is 8 years old will not have big breasts because she started earlier than some of her friends. She will have small, medium or large breasts depending on her genes and her weight.

How Breasts Make Milk

Inside a woman's breasts are tiny pockets called alveoli where milk is made by special milk-making cells. After a woman gives birth to a baby, hormones tell her alveoli to make milk. When a mother holds her baby next to her breast, the baby starts to suck on her nipple. The sucking draws the milk from the alveoli, through the milk ducts and out small holes in the nipple. The mother will keep making milk as long as she breast-feeds (nurses) her baby. When a mother stops breast-feeding her baby, her breasts stop making milk. Cool, eh?

fat cells

alveoli

areola

nipple

main duct

What Breasts Look Like

Breasts come in different sizes, shapes and colors. There is no perfect shape or size of breast.

As breasts grow so do a few hairs around the nipple—this is supposed to happen. Many girls have one breast that is bigger than the other, or two nipples that look different. Within two years of growth most breasts will balance out and look more or less the same, but not identical. (Most people have one foot that is slightly larger than the other, too.)

Some girls worry if their nipples are "innies" instead of "outies." This, too, is common. Some girls are concerned if their breasts feel lumpy because they worry about breast cancer. Cancer of the breast in girls is very rare. Many breasts feel lumpy all over. But if you are worried you can have a health professional check it out.

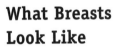

Developing Breasts

    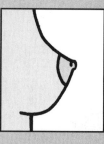

Stage 1.
In the beginning, girls, like boys, are flat chested.

Stage 2.
Some girls feel a tingling or soreness in their chests. A small bump under the nipple is called a breast bud.

Stage 3.
The breasts are rounder, and the nipples are bigger and darker. Nipples may be many colors, from light pink to dusky purple.

Stage 4.
The breasts are a little cone-shaped. Most girls start to menstruate sometime around now.

Stage 5.
Development complete—each girl is a work of art!

Wearing a Bra

It used to be that everyone had to wear a bra, and there were not very many types. Now girls have more choice. Some prefer a fitted undershirt or camisole. Some like to wear a bra all the time, even to bed (not a good idea). Once your breasts have begun to develop, when you play sports or exercise, a sports bra is a good idea for comfort and support.

Some bras are sized small, medium or large. Choose a bra like this the same way you would buy a T-shirt. Other bras have more shape and need to be fitted. Yes, it's best to get some help with this! A clerk at the store will measure the distance (in inches) from your back around to your chest at the fullest part of your breasts. This measurement is the number part of your bra size, for example 28, 30, 34... The cup size—AA, A, B, C, D—depends on how full your breasts are. Try on lots of bras to find the makes and styles that fit you best. It's important to get the right bra size as you continue to grow.

Breast Size

Like flowers in the spring our body grows in its own time and its own way.

While all breasts are beautiful, we often learn not to like what we have. Some girls may try to change their size. Exercising or massaging your breasts with special lotions won't make them bigger. Some girls are afraid to sleep on their stomachs just in case it prevents breast development. Putting on a bra that is too small will not make breasts smaller. And nothing will make breasts develop before your body gets the message that puberty has begun.

Nature doesn't care about the size of breasts. Big, small and medium breasts are all sensitive to touch and will produce enough milk to feed a baby if the time comes.

Feelings about Breasts

Breasts are an obvious sign that a girl is growing into a woman. Sometimes boys, and other girls, don't know how to act. They might make remarks about the size of your breasts. They sometimes talk loudly about girls who are "stacked" or "flat as a pancake."

Some boys, and even grown men, might try to rub against you or touch your breasts when they walk by. They have no right to do this. They aren't thinking about your feelings and may not care about or understand your embarrassment. You can say, "I don't like it when you talk that way or do that," or even a forceful, "Stop it." Even though you may feel embarrassed, talk to an adult if you continue to be harassed.

Hair

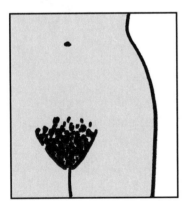

Pubic hair is the kinky hair that grows over the pubic bone and around the vulva. At first you'll notice a few straight hairs growing in new places. As you get more and more pubic hair, it will become thicker and form into a triangular shape.

As with the rest of your body hair, you might grow lots of pubic hair, or you might have hardly any. And your pubic hair might be a different color than the hair on your head.

Most girls develop underarm hair after they get pubic hair. You may also notice that the hair on your upper lip, arms and legs becomes darker and thicker.

Unfortunately, our society makes a big deal about body hair. The amount of body hair that you grow has to do with genetics. Some girls just have more hair than others, just like some guys have less than others.

Getting Rid of Unwanted Hair

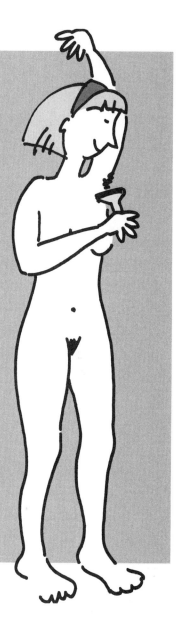

You have the choice of leaving your body hair to grow naturally or removing some of it. Many women get rid of the hair on their legs and around the "bikini line" of their upper thighs and lower abdomen by shaving or waxing. They also use chemical creams and bleaches to lighten the color of the hair on their upper lip and arms. It's not a good idea to pluck or shave the hair around your nipples, on your upper lip or around your vulva. The hair will grow coarser, or you might get an infection.

If you shave your legs or underarms, make sure the hair is softened with lots of soapy water or lotion. Use a sharp razor and gently pull the razor blade along your skin in the opposite direction that the hair grows. Never share a razor with another person because there is a risk of spreading viruses such as hepatitis C.

If you want to try a hot wax, go to a shop that provides this, since it is easy to burn yourself. Hot wax is painted on the hair you want removed. It cools and then it is ripped off, tearing the hair with it (ouch!).

Bleaching hair on your upper lip and thighs, with a product made for that purpose, can be done at home. It makes hair less noticeable, without the discomfort and cost involved with other methods. The beauty counter staff can tell you more about the range of products.

5 Menstruation

Your Period

There are many names for the same thing—your monthly cycle, your period, menstruation, your "friend," being on the rag, your moon time... Most girls start their period between the ages of 10 and 14. Once you start to get your period, you can conceive a baby—get pregnant—if you have sexual intercourse. Our periods stop at *menopause,* when we are in our late 40s or 50s.

"Menstruation" comes from the Latin word *mensis*, meaning "monthly." For most girls the length of time between the first day of one period and the first day of the next is 28 days (four weeks). But many girls have periods that start 20 to 35 days apart.

The number of days your period lasts is different for different girls, too. Most periods last about four days, but it is not unusual for girls to have periods as short as two days or as long as eight days. In the first year or two of menstruating, your periods may not be regular because your hormones are not into a set rhythm yet. If you are very excited or worried about something, or if you are exercising heavily or eating very little, it is common to miss a period.

Girls usually start their periods after their breasts have started to develop and they have some pubic hair and underarm hair. You may notice a whitish fluid secreted from your vagina a year or two before your period begins. When you change at night you may think, "What's *that* on the inside of my underpants?" This fluid lets you know that your vagina is cleaning itself (just like tears clean your eyes) and that the cervix is starting to do its job. "Where's my cervix?" you ask. See the diagram on page 11.

A girl who hasn't been told about periods might be frightened and think she has cut or injured herself. But when you menstruate, you're not bleeding in the way you do from a cut. Your body is shedding a thin layer of special blood and tissue from the uterus.

How Will I Know When I'm Going to Get It?

One day you will see a brown or reddish discharge on your underpants, or notice a small amount of blood in the toilet water or on the toilet paper. Or you might get a damp feeling in your underwear. You don't actually feel the menstrual flow happening. In the first couple of hours of your period, it is rare to have a gush of menstrual flow that stains your outer clothes.

The discharge you see when you get your period is made up of small amounts of blood and special tissue from your uterus. As your flow increases, it becomes brighter red. After a few days, it becomes a slight brownish discharge. It may seem like you are losing a lot of blood, but the total amount of menstrual flow is usually only a few tablespoons (50–100 ml).

Why Does It Happen?

You were born with all the ova or eggs you will ever need inside your two ovaries. There are hundreds of thousands of them. One egg is called an ovum. Until puberty the eggs are immature. At puberty, hormones make your eggs ripen. Once a month, an egg starts to mature. Usually only one ovum matures at a time, but sometimes two or more eggs ripen. Your ovaries take turns producing an egg.

Several days before the egg is released, girls may notice a sort of clear slippery fluid on their underwear or on the toilet paper after they've urinated (for some, this may not be noticeable until they have had their periods for a while). This sperm-friendly fluid or discharge (nice term!) is made by the cervix several days before the egg is released in order to give the sperm a greater chance of surviving while they wait for the egg to show up. The cool thing is, you can count on getting your period 12 to 14 days after you notice this fluid.

When the egg is ripe, it bursts out of the ovary. This is called *ovulation*. Some girls feel a little twinge when this happens, but most girls don't even notice it. After the egg is released, it travels from the ovary through the fallopian tube to the uterus. At the same time, the lining of the uterus thickens, in case the egg gets fertilized.

If the egg is fertilized by a sperm on its way to the uterus, a new life has started. The embryo will start to grow in the uterus, and will need the thick, nourishing lining of the uterus. So a woman won't get her period while she is pregnant. If the egg is *not* fertilized it dissolves within 24 hours and there is no need for the nourishing lining. So the uterus gets rid of it. This is called menstruation. The cycle is repeated about once a month.

Ovulation

Menstruation

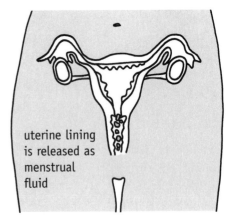

egg released into fallopian tube

uterine lining is released as menstrual fluid

Many girls get into the habit of circling on their calendars the day their period starts. It's helpful to know when you are expecting your period. If you miss a period, you'll know how long it has been since you last menstruated. This is particularly useful for those women who wonder if they're pregnant.

How Does It Feel?

Some girls don't notice any physical or emotional changes when they get their period. However, others find their menstrual cycles have as many dips as a roller coaster ride. You might have a surge of energy mid-cycle. On the other hand, you might not feel "yourself" at some point in the two weeks before you get your period. This is referred to as *PMS*, or *premenstrual syndrome*. When you are young PMS does not happen as noticeably—phew!

During your period you may not feel at all different. Or you might have cramps—a tightening of the uterine muscles deep inside your abdomen. Cramps can feel like an annoying twinge, or they can be very painful. Some young women also feel sick to their stomach.

a good question!

"My mom says she has PMS when she gets cranky. What does that mean?"
—GRADE 7 STUDENT

PMS stands for premenstrual syndrome. A syndrome is a bunch of physical symptoms that usually occur together—a person may experience one or many of the symptoms. When a female's hormones fluctuate during her menstrual cycle it affects many parts of her, not just her uterus. Her breasts may become sore and puffy, and she may get more pimples, feel "fat," be more tearful or feel easily irritated. The emotional effects of PMS can range from mild to extreme, with some women not noticing any change at all.

Girls who have severe menstrual cramps have extra hormones called prostaglandins, which cause the painful cramps. Lying down with a heating pad can help, as can light exercise. There are natural remedies you can try or your doctor can prescribe pills to make you more comfortable.

Protection!

To absorb your menstrual flow you can wear a sanitary napkin or pad, made from an absorbent material that attaches to your underpants. Tampons, which are made of compressed cotton, can also be used. They fit snugly inside your vagina.

Once you start developing breasts and have pubic hair, it's a good idea to carry a pad in your backpack or purse, just in case. Most public washrooms sell pads and tampons in a coin box on the wall. Keep some change handy in case you need one.

If you are at school, at camp or at a friend's house, then a teacher, nurse or parent will help you find a pad or tampon. If your menstrual flow has leaked through your underwear, you could wrap a sweatshirt or jacket around your waist so it covers the spot until you can change.

Menstrual flow has no odor (smell) when it leaves your body. But once out of the body, it starts to develop a strong odor. You can avoid this by changing your pad every three or four hours. Taking a bath or shower when you have your period can keep you feeling fresh.

If you have blood on your clothes or underwear, the stains will come out easier if you soak them in cold water and put them through a regular wash.

Pads

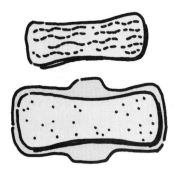

Sanitary pads are self-adhesive, like stick-it notes. Remove the wrapper, if there is one, and throw it in the garbage—not down the toilet, since it could clog the pipes. Peel off the paper to expose the sticky strip. Put the pad, sticky-side down, on the inside of your underpants. Unless you are wearing a bathing suit or very tight clothes, it is not possible for anyone to see that you're wearing a pad. While there are pads made for thongs, they are totally impractical, so stick with regular undies!

Depending on how heavy your flow is you'll need to change your pad every two to eight hours. When you change your pad, remove it from your underpants, fold it in half and wrap it in tissues or toilet paper.

Dispose of it in the special receptacle in a public washroom or in a garbage can at home. NEVER flush a pad down the toilet.

There are tons of different kinds of pads. They are different thicknesses, lengths and widths, and are made of different materials. Buy a variety and experiment with what works for you. The longer ones are good to wear through the night to avoid "leaks." Many people prefer 100 percent cotton pads that are not chemically bleached. These, as well as reusable cloth products, are available at health food stores. You'll notice "scented" pads—avoid all of these products as they use strong chemicals that can cause irritation. Anyway, who wants their crotch to smell like a flower shop?

Using a Tampon

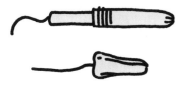

While pads are easy to figure out, using a tampon takes a bit more information. A tampon—especially the junior, slender models designed for girls—will slip into most vaginal openings. If your hymen has only a small opening, you might try using your fingers to gently stretch the opening wider (see more on hymens on page 12). This does not mean you are no longer a virgin. A virgin is someone who has never had sexual intercourse.

Most girls find there are many advantages to using tampons: they may be the only things around if you get your period unexpectedly, they are easy to carry, and they can be worn with tight pants, dance wear and bathing suits—you can't swim using a pad!

As with pads, there are different types of tampons, including:
- those with or without applicators
- those with applicators made of plastic or smooth cardboard
- those made from 100 percent cotton, non-dioxin material or the regular kind
- sizes varying from slender (thin) to super-absorbent (big)
- scented or unscented (avoid the scented ones)

So how do you use them? First, if there is a wrapper on the tampon remove it—obvious but important! If you've never checked yourself out, take a hand mirror and locate the opening to the vagina. It's the only opening that you can easily insert your finger into a ways.

Put one foot up on the edge of the toilet or tub. With one hand, gently hold back the folds of skin from around the opening. With your other hand, push the applicator or tampon into your vagina as far as it will comfortably go.

Sometimes the muscles in your vagina will feel as if they are tightening. Take a deep breath and relax. Remember, the vagina can stretch to let a baby pass through it, so a tampon should be no problem!

Aim the tampon toward the small of your back. Your vagina does not sit straight up and down in your body. It is angled backward.

If you are using a tampon with an applicator, push the plunger part

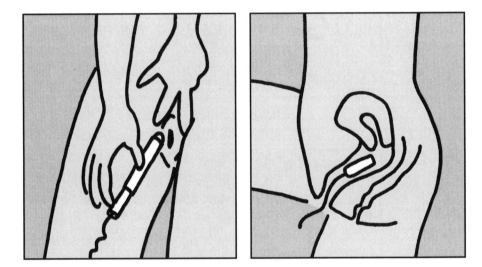

in all the way once the applicator is in your vagina. The tampon will push out of the applicator further into your vagina. Slip out the applicator and throw it away. Some paper applicators can be flushed.

If your tampon has no applicator, gently push the tampon into your vagina as far as your finger allows. It is now in place.

If your tampon is inserted properly, you won't be able to feel it. Amazing really! If it's not inserted far enough, you'll think, "Well *this* is not very comfortable." And you'll be walking like you just got off a horse! Relax, and push it further in until you can't feel it anymore. Ta da!

Never flush a pad or tampon unless you can pay for the plumber's bill!

The tampon cannot get lost. It won't pop out of your ear or anything. It has nowhere to go, and the opening to your cervix is far too small for it to travel through.

All tampons have strings, which should hang outside your body. When it is time to remove your tampon, gently pull on the string. If the string is tucked up where you can't feel it, simply slip your fingers around the end of the tampon and tug. It will slip out easily unless your vagina has become dry because there is no menstrual blood left. In this case, tug harder and it will come out...but you want to avoid this situation. Wrap the tampon in toilet paper and put it in the garbage. Don't flush them—ever.

Sometimes it is hard to know when to replace a tampon. Some girls replace it every time they go to the bathroom, or if they notice some menstrual spotting on their underwear or panty liner. If you are changing your tampon more than every three hours, then you likely need a tampon that absorbs more flow. Leaving a tampon in for longer than four hours can be dangerous, since the blood can be a breeding ground for germs. You should not wear a tampon at night unless you get up to change it. For girls with heavy periods, wearing a pad and a tampon at the same time can help.

Near the end of your period, when the blood becomes brownish, use a panty liner instead of a tampon. This way, you won't forget about the tampon.

Toxic Shock Syndrome

Toxic shock syndrome (TSS) is a rare but serious infection caused by a germ that gets into the bloodstream. It can affect anybody in certain situations, male or female. In the past super-absorbent tampons made of mixed materials came with directions that they could be worn for many hours. Now we know that it's not healthy to leave a tampon in for more than about four hours. If you experience a sudden high fever, vomiting and/or dizziness, remove your tampon and see a doctor immediately.

Douching

A douche is a cleanser sprayed into the vagina. Nobody needs a douche—nor does anyone need a deodorant for their genitals. Douches and sprays are unhealthy for the delicate vaginal area. If you shower or bathe everyday, you will be clean. Your vagina is always cleaning and moisturizing itself with fluid. Our mouth and eyes do the same thing.

Vaginal Fluids

When a girl is sexually excited (horny in slang terms) or thinking about something romantic, her vagina will become wet and slippery with fluid that comes from glands inside her vagina. There's no need to worry about that discharge, the slippery discharge you get a couple of weeks before your period or the sticky whitish stuff you see in your underpants.

If, however, you have a discharge that is yellow or greenish, thick like cottage cheese, foul-smelling or very itchy, then you have an infection. It's important to see a health professional about a vaginal infection before you start treating yourself with medication. For instance, a *yeast infection* is an overgrowth of something that's in the vagina to keep it healthy. It can grow out of control for many reasons: use of some soaps and bubble baths, wearing nylon underwear or a wet bathing suit, by wiping from back to front after a bowel movement, or taking certain antibiotics. The health professional will take a swab (a sample) of the infection to tell what it is and give you medicine or suggestions to help clear up the problem.

There are also *STIs* or *sexually transmitted infections*, which are passed from an infected person to their partner during genital contact, including sexual intercourse. You can read more about these in Chapter 9.

Pelvic Examinations

Unless a girl is having sexual intercourse, or having major problems with menstruation (such as very heavy bleeding or painful cramping), there is no need to have an examination of the inside of her vagina and her cervix. This is called a pelvic examination or, commonly, an internal.

You should, however, have a pelvic examination once a year after you have started having sex or whenever you think you might have an infection.

Many girls think a pelvic examination will hurt or be embarrassing. It shouldn't hurt, although it can be a little uncomfortable. Go to a health professional you feel comfortable with and ask them to explain what they are doing as they go along. The exam usually only takes a few minutes.

If you do not have a female physician, feel free to ask to have another woman in the room with you during a pelvic exam. If you get an uneasy feeling at any time, you can always say, "I think I'll do this another time, thanks."

6 Growing Up

From the moment you started life, you were growing. At puberty, hormones start to control your body shape. As you know, there are other factors that influence how your body will grow. How much and what kinds of food you eat, how physically active you are and how much sleep you get all affect your development.

About Bones

The long bones of your body—arm bones, leg bones, finger and toe bones—have rubbery cartilage at each end. It grows and makes your bones longer. At puberty, testosterone makes the cartilage grow quickly and then stop. This period of quick growth is called a growth spurt.

By the time puberty is over, there is a small cushion of cartilage at the ends of your bones. The rest of the bone is hard. When that happens, you stop growing taller.

Getting Taller

WEIRD!

As you know from looking around, women come in all different heights. When you are growing at your fastest, you will add about 2 to 4 inches (5 to 10 cm) in one year. No wonder your pants start to look too short! Girls usually start their growth spurt when they are about 10 or 11 years old, while most boys start around the age of 12 or 13. Most girls finish growing by age 16, while guys continue to grow until they are about 18.

If you start getting taller early, it does not mean you'll be a giant when you're older. You will grow only as tall as you are meant to grow, depending on the genes you have inherited.

Your body won't grow at the same rate all over. Your feet might suddenly grow two sizes. Then your hands will get bigger. Your face gets longer. Your chin and nose stick out more, and your hairline moves back. Your pelvic bones widen. Your other bones lengthen and you develop more muscles and fat. You might feel like some weird cartoon character who keeps being redrawn!

Diet and Exercise

Fat is the way the body stores energy. During puberty, all of this changing uses up a lot of energy. This is why you will notice an increase in your appetite. You start to open the fridge door to see what's there more often! If you are starting your growth spurt, you'll need that extra food energy for strong bones and muscles.

Eating for Health and Fun

You've heard about healthy eating, but what does it mean? No fries or hamburgers? No sweets? No. It means eating a variety of foods and cutting down on sugar, fried foods, fatty foods and salt.

Unlike many adults, you probably don't go around thinking, "Oh, this is full of fiber so I'll have lots of it." But it is good to have some idea of what healthy eating looks like. You probably know that it's a good idea to

Breakfast

Can you pick the best breakfast for a teenage girl?

1. One fried egg, two strips of bacon, a glass of orange juice, a glass of milk and one slice of whole-wheat bread with butter and jam.
2. Two slices of leftover pizza (extra cheese, mushrooms and green peppers) with a glass of juice (not a fruit "drink").
3. A bowl of cereal with raisins and enriched rice milk, a slice of cantaloupe and a glass of orange juice with calcium.
4. Hot chocolate with milk (not water), and a bagel with peanut butter and banana.

ANSWER: All of these breakfasts have a variety of foods that you need—breads or cereals, fruits or veggies, and some meat or alternatives. Breakfast 1 is not a good choice for every day because the butter and bacon add extra fat that you don't need.

The Question of Calcium

Which one of the following gives you the amount of calcium needed each day by a girl going through puberty?

1. Four glasses of milk.
2. Four glasses of fortified soy drink.
3. A large piece of cheddar cheese and a milkshake made with two glasses of milk and one scoop of ice cream.

ANSWER: All of them! Because your bones are growing, you need more calcium than children and adults.

eat a variety of foods—milk products such as milk, yogurt and ice cream; fresh fruits and vegetables; pasta, rice, bread and cereal; and meat protein, or alternatives such as tofu, beans and nuts. If you have a choice, pick the more intense colored vegetables such as spinach, broccoli, carrots and squash, and orange fruits such as cantaloupe and oranges. And instead of just grabbing high-fat snacks such as chocolate bars and potato chips, pick a handful of nuts, a bowl of popcorn (maybe with a sprinkling of cheese), carrot sticks or some yogurt.

If you're always feeling hungry, resist reaching for a quick fix like cookies. Try to eat more protein as well as more rice, noodles, potatoes or pasta, and whole-grain breads at your meals.

What about Sleep?

Do you yawn through most of your classes and fall asleep late at night watching TV? Chances are you are not getting enough sleep. Your body needs to be both active and get enough sleep to feel healthy and alert. While it's true that different people need different amounts of sleep, some doctors recommend adolescents get 10 hours of sleep each night.

This can be hard as you get older—you'll find that you want to stay up later and later, but you still need to get up for school! You have to find a balance. If you're tired all the time it could be your diet, activity level, emotional state—or lack of time in the sack! If your parents have a set bedtime for you, but you toss and turn because you're not tired and you wake up before the alarm goes off, perhaps you can talk about a later bedtime.

About Exercise

It doesn't matter what kind of exercise you choose—a team sport, biking, walking, dancing, swimming, skating—as long as you do something. Your bones and muscles need exercise to grow properly. Lots of kids find that exercise helps them think more clearly and better handle all the stresses of school, friendships and family. Girls who participate in a physical activity find they don't get bored as often as kids who hang around with "nothing to do."

Your Body Image

Every day you need at least 90 minutes of physical activity. How much do you get?

Body image means what *you* think about *your* body. Our bodies are ALL amazing and, as you know, all very different (what a boring world it would be if this was not the case). But what really matters is whether you can appreciate what you have. Many girls look at their bodies and think they are too fat. But are they? There is no ideal weight. How much you weigh depends on your height, your heredity, your gender, your health, your body type, your diet and your activity level. Most girls your age are fairly healthy, spend a bit too much time sitting on their seats, but do not have a weight problem. Still, compared to the girls we see on TV and in magazines, you may have more of a tummy, larger breasts or bigger thighs. Instead of feeling that we are okay just the way we are, we often look to media stars as an ideal.

Some girls don't like the fact that they are thin with small breasts. And some girls think that being skinny is best. There is no "best." If we

What's Your Strength?

Girls and guys have different strengths after they've gone through puberty. Everyone knows that guys put on more muscle, so that compared to a girl of the same height, weight and build, he would be able to lift more weight and run faster. But girls have their own strength. It's called *adipose* tissue—also known as fat. What does it do? Well, fat is the storage of energy in our body. And because females need more energy for breast-feeding and caring for a newborn, they store more adipose tissue on their upper arms, breasts, thighs and butt. This means that a girl can survive things a guy who is her equivalent couldn't. She could survive extreme drought and hunger, extreme heat and cold. It's just a different kind of strength.

are healthy but have learned not to like ourselves we can unlearn some of that by reminding ourselves every time we look into a mirror, "I am me, I am unique."

How Can You Tell If You're Too Thin or Too Fat?

While many young people are fine just the way they are, those who are too thin or very overweight can have serious health problems. So how do you know if you're a healthy weight?

If you can't shop in the same stores as your friends because there is nothing large enough, then you are probably carrying too much extra weight. If you can't stop eating even when you're full, then you may have an eating problem. But if you are the only one who thinks you are fat, then the problem probably isn't extra weight.

On the other hand, if everyone tells you to eat more because you're too skinny and you keep buying clothes in smaller sizes instead of larger sizes, you may be underweight. If you don't eat even though you're hungry, you should be asking yourself what's going on. If you think that you or a friend may have a problem with body image or eating, please consider talking to an adult who knows about this aspect of health or try contacting a phone help line. Check out For More Information on page 59.

Pimples and Acne

Zits. Everyone would prefer to avoid them, but nearly everyone gets them at some point. During the teen years your skin produces more oil, so you have to live through a "shiny face" and greasier hair stage. What kind of skin you have mainly depends on—you guessed it—heredity, just like your eye color and height. Let's look at why pimples or *acne* happens and what can be done about it.

When a skin pore becomes clogged with *sebum*—an oily substance made under the skin—a blackhead forms. When sebum gets trapped beneath the surface of the pore, you get a whitehead. When a whitehead becomes infected, it turns red and fills with pus—a pimple is born. A serious case of blackheads, whiteheads or pimples is called acne.

There is no guaranteed way to prevent pimples and acne. Squeezing pimples can make the problem worse by causing an infection or scarring. The pimple creams and lotions you see advertised on TV help dry up pimples once you've got them, but they don't prevent acne. Wash your face gently with a pure soap—one without perfumes and additives—rinse and dry it well. But don't overdo it. Doctors used to tell teenagers to stop eating greasy food such as fries, but this is not the cause of pimples. Eating healthy foods, drinking lots of water, getting enough sleep and exercise daily and avoiding cigarettes all lead to healthier skin, hair, nails and teeth. If your acne is causing you a lot of concern, a skin doctor (called a dermatologist) can give you prescription drugs to help the situation.

Skin and Sweat

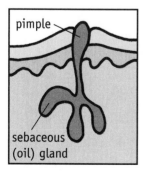

pimple

sebaceous (oil) gland

Did you know that skin is the largest organ of your body? And it does a lot of work. The top layer, the epidermis, is a protective layer of dead skin cells that flake off or need to be washed off. The sebaceous glands make an oily substance called sebum that gives skin its soft, stretchy feel. Sweat is your body's temperature regulator. It comes from millions of sweat glands all over your body.

During puberty, your body sweats more, produces more sebum and smells different. Your sweat smell changes because nature intended you to have a "sex smell" to attract males. Each person has an individual smell that can be pleasing to their partner. But that smell is different from body odor, which develops when the sweat stays around too long.

You will notice more sweat on your feet, on your palms (especially when you are nervous), under your arms and around your *groin*. When you perspire, the sweat clings to your skin and underarm hair. Bacteria are attracted to the warm moist areas; they start to grow and smell. But there's an easy solution! When you wash with soap and water, you remove the extra sweat, sebum and dead skin, and you kill the bacteria. Washing your favorite clothes more often is also important. Some people cover up the odor with deodorant and/or reduce the amount of sweating with antiperspirant.

Sweat itself doesn't smell—it's the bacteria growing in stale sweat that makes teachers open the windows for some air!

What Would You Do?

Sometimes, girls who are healthy and fit go on diets or eat less because they think it's the right thing to do. What would you do in these situations?

1. Your coach takes the co-ed team out for pizza after a game. You've been running for an hour and you're starving. In the change room all the girls talk about how hungry they are. When you get to the pizza place, the guys order the biggest pizza on the menu. Some of the girls order only a diet soft drink.

2. Your best friend is a gymnast and works out like crazy every day. She gives away her lunch and won't go out for treats. You notice that all her bones stick out and she tells you that she stopped getting her period. She thinks she's in great shape. You're worried that she's sick.

3. You find out that you're the only girl in your grade going out for the track team. You've been on the track team for two years, you're good and you enjoy it, but you don't want to look like a loner.

ANSWERS: There are no right and wrong answers. Chapter 8 gives some suggestions on how to make good decisions for yourself.

7 What Happens to Boys?

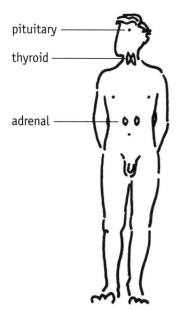

pituitary

thyroid

adrenal

Why bother to understand what guys go through at puberty? It's important for girls and boys to understand each other because we live in this world together! And while you've known since you were little that girls and boys are different, it's interesting to see how similar we are as well. Also, girls are often curious about the opposite sex.

Boys start puberty later than girls. And since the changes start in the genital area first, they are not very noticeable. Like girls, the changes boys go through take many years. Puberty starts, as it does for girls, when the pituitary gland sends a message to the sex glands to start making sex hormones. A boy's *testes* make the male sex hormone, testosterone, and small amounts of the female sex hormones, estrogen and progesterone. Boys' bodies make the same amounts of testosterone each day of the month, whereas girls' hormone levels rise and fall. Boys do not have a monthly cycle or anything similar to a period.

What Happens?

Which of these puberty changes happen only to boys?

- Get pimples
- Get wider shoulders
- Have a growth spurt
- Make sperm
- Get a period
- Get hair on the face
- Get pubic hair, underarm hair and darker leg hair

- Voice deepens
- Get bigger Adam's apples
- Grow breasts
- Develop wider hips
- Sweat more
- Get greasier hair and body odor
- Have more sexual thoughts

ANSWER: Only boys make sperm and get bigger Adam's apples and wider shoulders. Only girls get a period, grow breasts and develop wider hips. All the other changes of puberty happen to both boys and girls.

Puberty in Boys

Here are the main changes of puberty in boys:

Stage 1.
The *scrotum* (sac) gets bigger and more wrinkled. His *testicles* get bigger, and the skin on his penis gets darker. Pubic hair starts to grow. He sweats more and has a stronger odor. Mood swings start happening. His feet start to grow.

Stage 2.
His testicles and scrotum continue to grow. His penis gets larger. The pubic hair is darker and curlier. His voice starts to "crack"—gets high-pitched and then low-pitched. He has more spontaneous erections. In 60 percent of boys there are changes in breast tissue, swelling and tenderness (not permanent). He is more aware of his sexual feelings. The growth spurt starts.

Stage 3.
He keeps growing taller with wider shoulders and more muscles. He gets oilier hair and pimples (face, back...). His penis gets wider and his testicles start to make sperm. He can *ejaculate* semen. Hair grows in his underarms, as well as on his upper lip and chin.

Stage 4.
The shape of his skull and jaw changes so his face looks more mature. The Adam's apple is developed. His growing slows down. He grows thicker facial hair. Body hair will continue to increase for several more years.

What Is Sperm?

Male Sex Organs

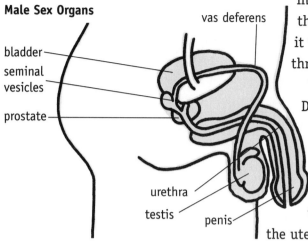

- vas deferens
- bladder
- seminal vesicles
- prostate
- urethra
- testis
- penis

During puberty a boy starts to make millions of sex cells, called sperm, inside his testes. He will make new sperm every day for the rest of his life. A sperm is so small you cannot see it without a microscope. It is made up of a head and a thread-like tail.

The new sperm takes four to six weeks to mature. During that time it travels through long, coiled tubes inside the testes (slang term—*balls*) and through the *vas deferens* to a storage area.

Sperm are slow and not very tough. They need to be mixed with a high-energy liquid, called semen, to swim and survive. Sperm must be able to swim up the uterus and to the fallopian tubes to fertilize an egg.

What Is an Erection?

Usually a boy's penis is soft and hangs close to his body. Sometimes, for no reason, or if he is thinking about something sexy or touching his genitals, his penis becomes hard. This is called an erection or, more commonly, a *boner* or hard-on. There is no bone in the human penis (unlike in some other mammals). The penis becomes stiff and stands out from the body because the spongy tissue inside fills with extra blood. A penis must be erect to enter the vagina during sex. While erections happen throughout a male's lifetime (even as a baby), they visit a guy more frequently during his teen years. As long as a boy is wearing underwear, people around him won't notice when his penis becomes hard.

Flaccid Penis

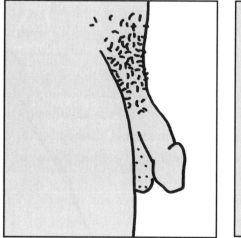

Erect Penis

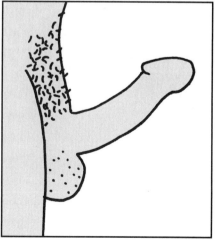

Circumcision

Boys are born with loose skin covering the end of their penis; this is called *foreskin*. Sometimes for religious or cultural traditions this is removed. The procedure, generally done on newborns, is called *circumcision*. It doesn't change the way the penis works, but it is why some penises have a rounded end and some look pointier.

About Ejaculation

During puberty, a boy makes and ejaculates semen for the first time. A very common word for semen and ejaculation is come or cum. Ejaculation can happen when a boy rubs his genitals (masturbates) or during his sleep. Ejaculation during sleep is called a wet dream. Males also ejaculate when they have sex. The intense feeling a boy has all over his body when he ejaculates is called an orgasm. An ejaculation is not the same thing as an orgasm, but most often they happen at the same time.

Do Boys Feel the Same Way As Girls?

While we look quite different on the outside, on the inside, guys and girls have much in common. Everyone is kind of excited about not being a little kid anymore. And boys often have the same kinds of worries as girls when they go through puberty. They worry about their size and their skin. They compare their penises and testicles to other boys' and worry that they are not big enough or don't look "normal." They wonder if they are attractive; they worry that nobody will like them. They may not understand all their sexual dreams and fantasies. They feel pressure to be cool. Guys who do not seem tough enough are often bullied and called "gay" or "faggot." This sometimes makes boys do things and say things just to "fit in." Girls also feel pressure to "fit in," but in a different way. It's important to remember that everyone has lousy days as well as amazing days, no matter what gender you are!

a good question!

"Why do girls have to physically go through much more than guys at puberty?"
—GRADE 6 GIRL

Because we are the lucky ones who sometimes get to have the amazing experience of being pregnant and breast-feeding a baby!

8 Making Decisions

Having to make decisions is part of life; it also helps you become more mature. And while some decisions are easy to make—like doing up your coat when it's cold out (or not)—others are tough. It takes practice and learning from our mistakes and successes to get good at making the decisions that are best for us.

Ways to Make Decisions

Different people make decisions in different ways. Even one person may make decisions differently from one situation to the next. So what's the best way to decide something? Let's look at a couple of examples.

1. After school your friends ask if you're going to hang out with them. You really want to, but you had agreed to go home right away. How do you decide what to do? What do you think you would decide? How long would it take to make a decision?

Here are three different ways that a decision could be made. After reading these, go back and rethink your answers to the questions above.

- *Weigh the consequences: "I don't know, I guess it would mostly depend on how much trouble I'd get into if I didn't show up at home."*—K.L., age 16

   What will you miss if you don't go with your friends? How much time have you spent with them lately? How much trouble will you get in at home? Would there be any point trying to call your parents and negotiate? What happened the last time you did not follow through with an agreement?

- *Go on impulse: "It's easy in this case to, like, just say 'Sure!' and not really think about it much."*—Jessie, age 13

  You could simply follow your first impulse or thought. This would result in an immediate decision one way or the other.

- *Let someone else decide: "I guess I'd call my mom and see if it was okay with her."*—E.M., age 10

  You could let someone else decide. In this case you might say to your friends, "I don't know, I'm supposed to go right home." If they say, "Okay, see you later," you go with that. If they say, "Oh, come on, just for a while," you go with that. If you call your parents and they say, "Okay" or "No," you go with that.

Let's try another couple of situations using these three kinds of decision-making.

2. You have been going out with someone for a couple of months. You really like each other. You've kissed and touched on top of your clothes. You're curious to do more, but you don't know if you're ready, or if he's ready.

- *Weigh the consequences:* You can try to figure out what might happen if you go further. Would you just do it or hint about it first? What if it went further than you wanted? What if the other person thought you were weird for doing it or for deciding to wait? What if other kids found out?

- *Go on impulse:* You don't spend any time thinking about it—you just react to how you are feeling at the moment. This could include many feelings, such as scared, horny, cautious, curious...

- *Let someone else decide:* You could let the other person make all the moves and just go along with it, or you could follow what adults in your life may have told you (for instance, to wait until you are older). You could talk with a friend, sibling or trusted adult and go with what they suggest.

What do you think you would do? How would you decide? How long would it take you to decide?

3. You're hanging out with some new friends. Someone takes out a pack of cigarettes and asks you if you want one. You don't smoke, but you're tempted to take one.

- *Weigh the consequences:* What if someone sees you? What will your friends think if you say "No"? What if you don't smoke it right? What if you like it and start smoking?

- *Go on impulse:* You just do the first thing you feel based on curiosity, or what you've been taught, or wanting to be part of the group, or wanting to be different...

- *Let someone else decide:* You go along with what another person in the group says. For instance, "Smoking is stupid, don't do it," or "Come on, don't be a baby." You may also defer to another person by saying, "I have a deal with my dad that I won't smoke."

What do you think you would do? How would you decide? How long would it take you to make your decision?

4. Turn back to the situation involving the track team on page 42 and ask the same questions.

Making a decision is like dropping a stone into a pond. The ripples it

So What's Right?

creates in the water spread all the way out, touching everything in their path, long after the stone disappears. How you decide something affects you and the people in your life. You owe it to yourself to learn how to make the best decisions you can at a given time—and then learn from them.

All of the decisions you make would be based on your values (what's important to you), past experiences and how much practice you've had at making decisions. How long it takes to make a decision often depends on the type of decision you have to make. In examples 1 and 3 above, decisions are often made in seconds, but for number 2 the person may take more time.

Remember, you can almost always say, "I have to think about it." *If you're feeling rushed into something, it's hard to do what's right for you.*

Deciding what's right in a certain situation is not always easy. Do your best and later, if you see that it wasn't such a great choice, do what you can to fix it. It takes a lot of courage and wisdom to go back and say, "I don't think that was the best decision. I've changed my mind."

9 More about Sex

Attractions

Sexual attractions are a big part of growing up. When you're first going through puberty you may be hot for a musician, an actor, an older sibling's friend or even a teacher! Adults may call this a "crush." Often you never let the other person know about it, but it's fun to fantasize or daydream about being with them.

At some point it's likely that you will become attracted to someone whom you could actually be involved with. When you're around that person, you'll feel a bit sweaty and warm, you may become aware of new feelings in your genitals, you'll want to look good and you may be shyer or more rowdy than usual. If the other person likes you, the same things happen for them. There may be lots of online flirting and your ear will get hot from all the phone chats! It feels good and exciting to have someone like you. You just have to make sure you don't stop spending time with other friends or doing your work at home and school.

a good question!

"When I was in Grade 7 I was going out with this guy...it felt so awkward! Why?"
—M.M., AGE 18

At some point when two people like each other, they may feel pressure to say they are "going out," or some similar term. If you're in high school (and your parents don't forbid it), then one-to-one time can be comfortable. But before that, it's often just plain weird. What can be more comfortable at this earlier age is just hanging out in a group together. This way you can joke, flirt and get used to the whole romance thing without wondering what you should do together or how far to go sexually.

Relationships

Being in love and having a good relationship are not always the same thing. Think about the relationships you have with friends, family members or a boyfriend/girlfriend. Below, name four characteristics or things that are part of a healthy relationship.

- _____
- _____
- _____
- _____

You're on the right track if you put down some of the following points: honesty, trust, making each other laugh, shared values, similar interests, respect, not afraid to disagree, can solve problems together and, if sexual interest is part of the deal, the enjoyment of physical sharing—without high risks.

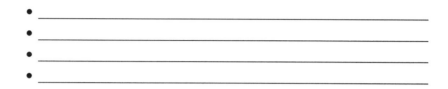

a good question!

"How do you know when you're in love?"
—SARAH, GRADE 9

Being in love is a feeling. You get excited or horny, you think about the person all the time, you feel a bit crazy... It can happen in an instant. Falling out of love can also happen in an instant. This can happen to people of all ages. Real *love* is a verb—an action word. It involves all parts of you. It takes time and doesn't just come or go.

More Than Kisses

There are laws about how old you have to be to have sexual intercourse. What's the age in your area?

Messing around, making out, touching—these are things teens may do when they are turned on but not ready for sexual intercourse. A very common and important question is, "When is the right time for sex?" What do you think? Do you know what your parents would say? Do you know what the law says?

Unlike what you see on TV, some young people do remain virgins until they're married. Some want to wait until finishing high school. Many say they'd wait until they "felt ready," which partly means being in a trusting relationship. Your parents will likely hope you are at least 30 years old! While no single opinion is right for everyone, youth who have intercourse before they turn 16 are much more likely to regret it, especially girls. Waiting until you are older is not always easy, but teens who have good information and goals for their future often make that choice.

Sexual Abuse

Internet Smarts

You probably already know this about Internet use, but just as a reminder...

- Don't believe everything you read!
- Keep your private information (real name, phone number, school, email and home address) to yourself unless a parent/adult gives you the okay.
- Tell a parent/adult if a stranger tries to talk you into giving out this information.
- If a pornography site pops up on your screen it can be tough to get rid of so explain to an adult what's up and get their help.

Sometimes girls and boys are forced, tricked or bribed into sexual touching or sexual activities, including being used for *pornography* (porn). The abuser is usually someone the child knows who is older or more powerful than they are. It may be a family member, friend of the family, neighbor, babysitter—anybody really. Any type of intimate sexual contact with children is called sexual abuse and it's illegal. Kids often wait until they are older before telling someone about the abuse.

There are many reasons for this:

- They may feel that it was their fault. It is *never* the child's fault, but the abuser may convince them that it is.
- They may have been threatened or bribed into keeping the secret.
- They may have just been very confused and embarrassed.
- They may have tried to tell someone but were not believed.

We all need to have positive, loving physical touch every day. Since sexual abuse doesn't always hurt physically, it can be confusing. If you have had anything sexual happen to you that made you feel uncomfortable, please speak to an adult about it. Teachers, camp counselors and child care and youth leaders are trained about abuse. They will reassure you that it was not your fault. Also, it's only when someone tells their secret that the abusers will be stopped. There are confidential phone lines (see page 59) you can call where you don't even have to give your name or phone number.

Sexual Assault

While we often hear in the news about teens being *sexually assaulted* when walking down the street at night or going into a building, the fact is that most assaults are carried out by people we know. Any **unwanted** sexual kissing or touching,

When someone is drunk they cannot give consent.

whether there is forced intercourse or not, is a form of sexual assault. That means there is no *consent*. Forced intercourse is often called *rape*. For teens and adults, the person who forces themselves on us is often someone we are involved with—perhaps someone we are going out with, living with or even married to.

Say you were with someone alone because you thought you wanted to make out a bit. They probably wouldn't need to use force. As with child sexual abuse, they may just use words. They may say, "You're so sexy, what are you going to do now that you've turned me on?" Or, "I thought you really liked me." Or girls may say to guys, "What's the matter, are you gay?"

Sometimes girls feel guilty when they end up doing something sexual that they didn't want to do. They think, "Maybe it's because of the way I was dressed. Maybe it's because we were alone. Maybe it's because I was drinking." The point is that even if a girl *might* have protected herself better, *she didn't commit the crime.*

If you have been involved with any form of sexual assault—please talk to someone about it. (See page 59.)

STIs

As you know from the other chapters, every time a male and female (before menopause) have sexual intercourse it can result in a pregnancy. The other thing all people, of all ages, who are having sex need to know about are sexually transmitted infections or STIs. They are also referred to as diseases (STDs). Let's look briefly at what these are, how you get them, how you know if you have one, what they can do to you and how to avoid them.

There are two basic kinds of STIs. The ones caused by bacteria can be cured with medication. Those caused by a virus can't be cured with medication but can be treated to reduce their effect on a person. Here are a few of the most common STIs:

Bacteria	Virus
Chlamydia	HPV (human papilloma virus)
Gonorrhea	Herpes
Syphilis	Hepatitis B
	HIV (human immunodeficiency virus)

How You Get Them

If you get an STI or experience genital irritation and then have unprotected sex, you have a much higher risk of getting HIV.

As the name says, these infections are passed or transmitted from one infected person to their partner during certain kinds of sexual contact. You don't get these through hugging, kissing or touching with your hands. Unprotected vaginal and *anal intercourse* (the anus is the bum hole) are the easiest forms of transmission.

While HIV (the virus that causes AIDS—acquired immune deficiency syndrome) is transmitted through unprotected sexual intercourse, there are other ways of getting it. It can easily be passed between people who share needles, including tattoo needles and the ink inside them. It can also be passed from an infected mother to her baby—although if the mother gets on special AIDS medication the chance of this happening is reduced.

How a Person Knows They Are Infected

When a person gets an STI, one of the problems is that they often don't know they have it. Some people do get symptoms (a symptom shows you have something—for example, a symptom of a cold is a runny nose). Those lucky enough to have a symptom may notice a discharge from the vagina or urethra, or sores or bumps on their genitals. Yuck!

However, many people never have obvious signs of illness. When a person gets HIV they can feel fine for *years* before noticing symptoms. So how can you know? The only way someone can know that they have an STI is to get tested at a clinic, although not all STIs are tested.

What Can STIs Do to You?

If a person has one of the bacterial infections, they can take antibiotics and be cured. If they are *not* treated, the infection could lead to more serious problems.

With the viruses there is good and bad news. Most young people these days are vaccinated against *hepatitis B*, so they probably won't get it. HPV can just cause bothersome wart-like bumps on the skin, but depending on the type and location, it can cause cancer of the cervix, especially for girls who have unprotected sex from an early age. Fortunately, our immune system can sometimes get rid of HPV on its own. Herpes—which is in the same family as the cold sores people get on their lips—can cause painful blisters on and around the genitals. For a pregnant woman, herpes can be extremely dangerous if it's passed on to her baby during the birth.

"What about oral sex? Can I still get an STI?"
—HIGHSCHOOL GRAD

Oral sex, which goes by many slang terms including "going down" and "*blow jobs*," means putting the mouth on another person's genitals. It is not possible to get pregnant through this form of sex, but it is possible to get and transmit STIs. Most youth count oral sex as a sexual activity.

What about AIDS?

When a person has HIV and then develops AIDS, their immune system is no longer working properly. This means that diseases their body would normally fight could end up killing them. Fortunately in many (but not all) countries, people can get medication that helps them live much longer. However, because of all the side effects, the medication itself is very hard to live with at times. And remember, you will not get HIV if you go to school with, live with or care for someone who has the disease.

Protection

The best way to avoid getting an STI is to avoid risky sexual activities. Not having sexual intercourse, often called abstinence, obviously reduces the chance of getting an infection. Hugging, kissing and touching with hands are all safe.

When people have sexual intercourse they can reduce the risk of getting an STI by using protection. You've got it—*condoms*. When used properly every time, condoms are very effective at stopping the spread of STIs, including HIV. There are other ways to make sex safer and it's the responsibility of anyone having sex to become well informed.

Birth Control

Most of the time, when a man and woman have sex, it is because it feels good, not because they want to make a baby. So unless they want a baby, every time a couple has intercourse they must use some form of birth control.

Condoms and *birth control* pills are two methods of protection commonly used by young people. The male condom, which is like a narrow balloon, is rolled down over the erect penis. It catches the semen (and any infected

The Morning-After Pill

Females who have had unprotected sexual intercourse can use an ECP—emergency contraceptive pill. It is also called the morning-after pill. It should be taken as soon as possible after unprotected sex, but can be used up to five days after. It doesn't work all the time.

fluid) before it enters the vagina. Birth control pills work mainly by stopping the egg from being released. They do not protect against STIs. There are other forms of birth control that use hormones as well. No method works 100 percent of the time—except not having sexual intercourse.

When a pregnancy does happen by accident, the girl or woman has three choices. She can carry on with the pregnancy and then either keep the baby or give it up for adoption. Or she can end the pregnancy with an abortion. None of these three options is easy, so it's highly recommended that young people who find themselves in this position talk to a trusted adult. As long as they don't worry about being punished, girls will often go to someone in their family. They can also go to a teen clinic, a teacher or call a hotline. See page 59 for more details.

Where to Go for More Help

We've given you some information about the sexual part of life, but you probably have many more questions. This a challenging and exciting time, with lots of changes. The following are some suggestions about where else to go for more info. In terms of Internet sites, when you are checking for puberty information, pornography sites may pop up on your computer. These sites can be nasty. Don't try to get out of the site, just turn off the screen and ask for help. Also, the computer you are working on may block any search that includes any sex-related words.

For More Information

Books

Kauchak, Therese. Real Beauty: 101 Ways to Feel Great about You. American Girl Library, 2004.

Wolf, Anthony. *Get Out of My Life—But First Could You Drive Me and Cheryl to the Mall?* New York: The Noonday Press, 1991.

Web Sites

www.kidshealth.org
In English and Spanish, for pre-teens, teens and parents. Many topics are covered.

www.sexualityandyou.ca
In English and French, for teens, parents and health educators.

www.teenwire.com
In English and Spanish, primarily for teens. Provided by Planned Parenthood of America.

Videos/Films

Changes series. National Film Board of Canada. Inexpensive, Grades 4–6.

It's a Girl's World. National Film Board of Canada. Excellent look at bullying, Grades 4–10.

Talking about Sex: A Guide for Parents. Planned Parenthood of America (1-800-669-0156).

Phone Hotlines

Kids Help Phone
1-800-668-6868 (in Canada)
Free and confidential—any topic.

Childhelp U.S.A.
1-800-422-4453 (in the United States)
Child abuse hotline.

Parents' Help Line
1-888-603-9100 (in Canada)
Professionals available for any topic.

You can also call your local public health or Planned Parenthood office for help.

Glossary

abortion *(uh-BORE-shun)*: a medical procedure to end a pregnancy.

acne *(AK-nee)*: a bad case of pimples.

adipose *(ADD-uh-pose)*: fatty tissue.

adolescence *(add-o-LESS-sens)*: the stage of life between childhood and adulthood.

adolescent *(add-o-LESS-sent)*: a person going through adolescence.

amniotic fluid *(am-nee-AH-tik FLOO-id)*: the liquid that surrounds the unborn baby in the uterus.

anal intercourse *(AY-nul IN-ter-kors)*: when the penis is inserted into the anus of a partner.

anorexia *(ah-nor-REX-ee-ah)*: a serious illness in which girls or boys starve themselves.

anus *(AY-nus)*: the opening where feces (poop) leaves the body.

areola *(ah-REE-oh-luh)*: the ring of skin around the nipple.

aroused *(ah-RAU-zd)*: feeling sexual excitement.

asshole *(AZ-hole)*: slang for anus.

balls *(BALZ)*: slang for testes.

birth control *(BURTH CON-troll)*: methods used to prevent pregnancy.

bisexual *(bye-SEX-shu-hul)*: an orientation or attraction toward both males and females.

bladder *(BLADD-her)*: a sac inside the body that holds urine.

blow job *(BLO jobb)*: slang for oral sex.

boner *(BOH-nur)*: slang for erection.

bowel movement *(BOW-ell MOOF-ment)*: solid waste that leaves through the anus.

breast *(BREST)*: the milk-producing glands of a woman, or the chest of a man.

cervix *(SIR-vicks)*: the lower part of the uterus.

cesarean *(si-ZAR-ee-en)*: surgical operation to remove a baby from the uterus.

circumcision *(sir-kum-SISH-un)*: the operation to remove the foreskin of the penis.

clitoris *(KLIT-or-is)*: a sensitive organ, seen on the outside above a girl's urinary opening.

come or cum *(CUHM)*: slang for semen and ejaculation.

conception *(kon-SEP-shun)*: the joining of the female egg and the male sperm to make a new life.

condom *(KON-dum)*: a tube made of latex rubber or other material that is rolled onto the penis before sexual intercourse to prevent disease and pregnancy.

consent *(KON-cent)*: to agree to something.

dick *(DIK)*: slang for penis.

discharge *(DISS-charj)*: fluid or mucus from a body opening or sore.

ejaculate *(ee-JACK-you-lat)*: semen.

ejaculation *(ee-JACK-you-lay-shun)*: when semen comes out of the penis.

embryo *(EM-bree-oh)*: the name for an unborn baby for the nine weeks after conception.

erection *(ee-REK-shun)*: when the penis fills with blood and becomes stiff and hard.

erotic *(ee-ROT-ick)*: books, movies or feelings about sexual matters.

estrogen *(ES-tro-jen)*: the female sex hormone made mainly in the ovaries.

fallopian tubes *(fuh-LOPE-ee-un)*: the narrow tubes between the ovaries and the uterus.

female *(FEE-mail)*: women, girls.

fertilization *(fur-till-eye-ZAY-shun)*: when the egg and sperm join to start a new life.

fetus *(FEET-us)*: the name for an unborn baby from nine weeks after conception until its birth.

flaccid *(FLA-sid)*: soft or limp.

fooling around *(FU-ling uh-ROWND)*: slang for sexual touching or sexual intercourse.

foreskin *(FOUR-skin)*: the skin around the head of the penis.

French kissing *(FRENCH KISS-sing)*: an open-month kiss with tongue-to-tongue contact.

gay *(GHAY)*: common word for a male homosexual.

gender *(JEN-duhr)*: being male or female.

genes *(JEANS)*: the part of each cell that carries inherited traits on to the next generation.

genitals *(JEN-a-tulls)*: the outside sex organs of both males and females.

glands *(GLAN-dz)*: a part of the body that makes secretions such as hormones and milk.

groin *(GROI-n)*: the area around the genitals.

hepatitis B *(HEP-uh-TIE-tiss bee)*: a virus that affects the liver; it can be spread by unprotected sex or shared needles.

heredity *(hair-ED-i-tee)*: the characteristics of your family that are passed to you at conception.

heterosexual *(HET-er-oh-SEK-shoo-ul)*: someone who is emotionally and sexually attracted to people of the opposite sex.

homosexual *(HOME-oh-SEK-shoo-ul)*: someone who is emotionally and sexually attracted to people of the same sex.

hormones *(HOAR-moans)*: chemical messengers that tell parts of your body to do something.

horny *(HOAR-nee)*: slang for being aroused or wanting sex.

hymen *(HI-mun)*: a ring of skin that may partly cover the vaginal opening.

jerking off or jacking off *(JURHK-king or JAKK-king)*: slang for masturbation.

labia *(LAY-bee-ah)*: the folds of skin around the opening of the vagina.

larynx *(LARR-inks)*: the part of the throat containing the vocal cords.

lesbian *(LEZ-bee-an)*: common word for a female homosexual.

lips—i.e., inner lips and outer lips *(LIPZ)*: other words for labia.

making out *(MAY-king out)*: slang for sexual touching.

male *(MAIL)*: men or boys.

mammary glands *(MA-muh-ree GLAN-dz)*: the milk-making glands in the breast.

masturbation *(mass-tur-BAY-shun)*: rubbing the genitals for sexual pleasure.

menopause *(MEHN-oh-paws)*: a woman's final menstrual period.

menstruation *(men-strew-AY-shun)*: the monthly shedding of the lining of the uterus.

miscarriage *(MISS-care-ridge)*: a spontaneous abortion of a fetus.

nipple *(NIP-pull)*: the small raised part in the center of the breast.

oral sex *(OR-ull seks)*: when one partner puts her mouth on the genitals of the other.

orgasm *(OR-gaz-um)*: an intense whole-body feeling at the height of sexual excitement.

orientation *(OR-ree-en-TAY-shun)*: whom a person is emotionally and sexually attracted to.

ova *(OH-vah)*: the female egg cells.

ovary *(OH-vah-ree)*: the gland that makes female sex hormones and egg cells.

ovulation *(OV-you-lay-shun)*: the release of a mature egg from the ovary.

penis *(PEE-niss)*: the tube-like sex organ of males that hangs outside their bodies.

period *(PEER-ee-id)*: menstruation.

pituitary gland *(pi-TYOU-uh-terr-ee)*: a gland in the brain that makes hormones.

placenta *(plah-SEN-tah)*: an organ that connects the mother to the unborn baby.

PMS or premenstrual syndrome *(PREE-mehn-strul)*: a group of physical and/or emotional changes some women experience 3 to 14 days before their period.

pornography *(por-NOG-ra-fee)*: images that have a sexual content and are intended to cause sexual arousal; also called "porn" or "adult entertainment."

pregnant *(PREGG-nunt)*: having an embryo or fetus growing in the uterus.

progesterone *(PRO-jes-ter-own)*: a female sex hormone.

puberty *(PEW-burr-tee)*: the physical and emotional changes during adolescence.

pubic hair *(PEW-bik)*: the hair that grows around the genitals.

rape *(RAYP)*: forced sexual intercourse.

reproduction *(ree-pro-DUCK-shun)*: creating life.

reproductive organs *(ree-pro-DUCK-tiv OR-guns)*: sex organs needed to make babies.

scrotum *(SKROW-tum)*: the soft sac in males that holds the testes.

sebum *(SEE-bum)*: the oily substance made in the sebaceous glands.

secretion *(suh-CREE-shun)*: a fluid that comes from the body.

semen *(SEE-mun)*: the whitish liquid that males ejaculate, made from sperm and fluid.

seminal vesicles *(SEM-i-nul VES-i-kuls)*: two structures that produce a fluid that helps make up semen in a male.

sex *(SEKS)*: male or female; also a common term for sexual intercourse.

sexual assault *(a-SAWLT)*: unwanted sexual contact, including rape.

sexual harassment *(huh-RASS-ment)*: being bothered by someone in a sexual way.

sexual intercourse *(IN-ter-kors)*: when the penis enters the vagina.

sexuality *(sek-shoo-AL-li-tee)*: feelings and attitudes about your sexual self.

sperm *(SPURM)*: the male sex cell needed to make a baby.

stillbirth *(STIHL-burth)*: when a baby is born after dying inside the uterus.

STIs or sexually transmitted infections *(in-FEX-shuns)*: germs that can be passed on during sexual activity.

straight *(STRATE)*: slang term for a heterosexual person.

sweat glands *(SWETT)*: the parts of your body that regulate body temperature.

testes *(TES-teez)*: the testicles.

testicles *(TES-ti-kuls)*: male sex glands that make sex hormones and sperm.

testis *(TES-tis)*: one testicle.

testosterone *(tes-TOS-tur-own)*: a male sex hormone.

transsexual or transgender *(tranz-SEKS-shul or tranz-JEN-duhr)*: also called "trans", people who cross the boundaries of the sex and/or gender they were given at time of birth.

umbilical cord *(um-BILL-i-cul)*: the cord connecting an unborn baby to the placenta.

urethra *(you-REE-thrah)*: the tube through which urine (and semen, in males) leaves the body.

urine *(YUR-in)*: body waste from the bladder—pee.

uterus *(YOU-ter-us)*: the organ that holds and nourishes an unborn baby, also called "womb."

vagina *(VAH-jeye-nah)*: the stretchy passageway of muscles that joins the uterus to the outside of the body.

vas deferens *(VAZ DEF-eh-renz)*: the small tube where sperm travel from the testicles.

vulva *(VUL-vah)*: the outside sex organs of a female.

yeast infection *(YEEST in-FEX-shun)*: an overgrowth of healthy organisms in the vagina that causes an unusual discharge and/or discomfort; it can be passed on during sex but is not an STI.

Index